MW01136656

Hello!
I am an OWL.

Owls live in forests, deserts, and even urban areas.

Owls can be found on almost every continent. This shows they can "adapt" to different places.

"Adapt" means we can change and adjust to fit in.

Barn owls got their names because they like to nest in *barns*.

Some owl species use abandoned nests of other birds.

In some cultures, owls are symbols of good luck.

Owls can fly silently due to special feathers that break up and absorb sound.

I can move through the air without making noise!

Owls are "apex predators", this means they are on the top of the food chain.

Owls are carnivores and mainly eat small mammals like mice and rats.

Snowy owls will travel long distances in search of food.

Small owls can be just 5 inches (12.7cm) tall and weigh 1.4oz (40g).

...but the great horned owl, can be over 2 feet (61cm) tall or 9lbs (4kg).

Owls have powerful night vision.

Owls have a special face shape that sends sound to their ears.

An owl's ears are "asymmetrical". That means that one is higher and one is lower.

With asymmetrical ears they can easily find prey.

During the daytime, owls may close their eyes or look like they are sleeping.

Owls often spend their days in hidden or sheltered spots.

Owls are covered in feathers, not fur.

Owls prefer to hunt and "roost" alone. Roosting is when a bird rests.

Owls usually only spend time together when they need a mate.

Owls groom each other's feathers.
This is called "preening".

The mother usually cares for the owlets in the nest. The father goes out hunting.

Owlets are born blind and featherless.

Owlets eat "regurgitated" food from their parent...

That means the parent chews up the food and then shares it with the owlet.

Owls communicate with hoots, screeches, and hisses.

Owls can live for more than 10 years in the wild.

Manufactured by Amazon.ca
Acheson, AB